T0042267

NATIONAL GEOGRAPHIC

It Can Fly

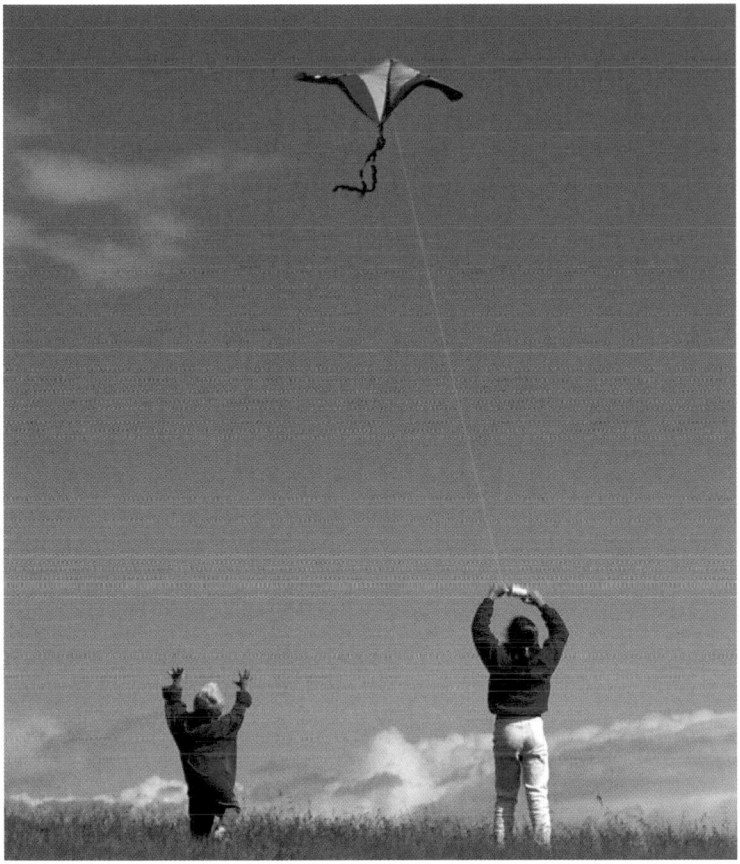

Kevin Biggs

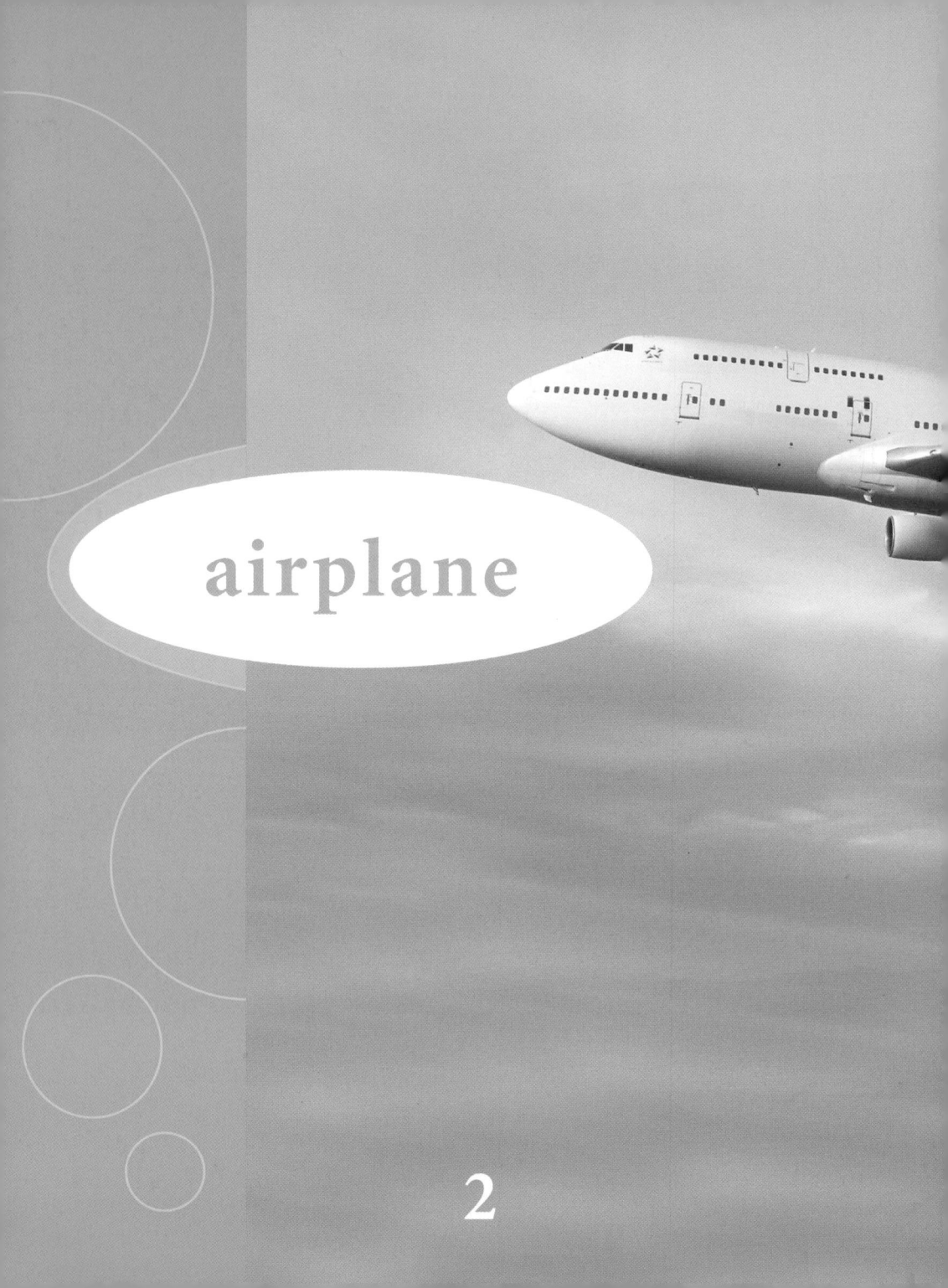
airplane
2

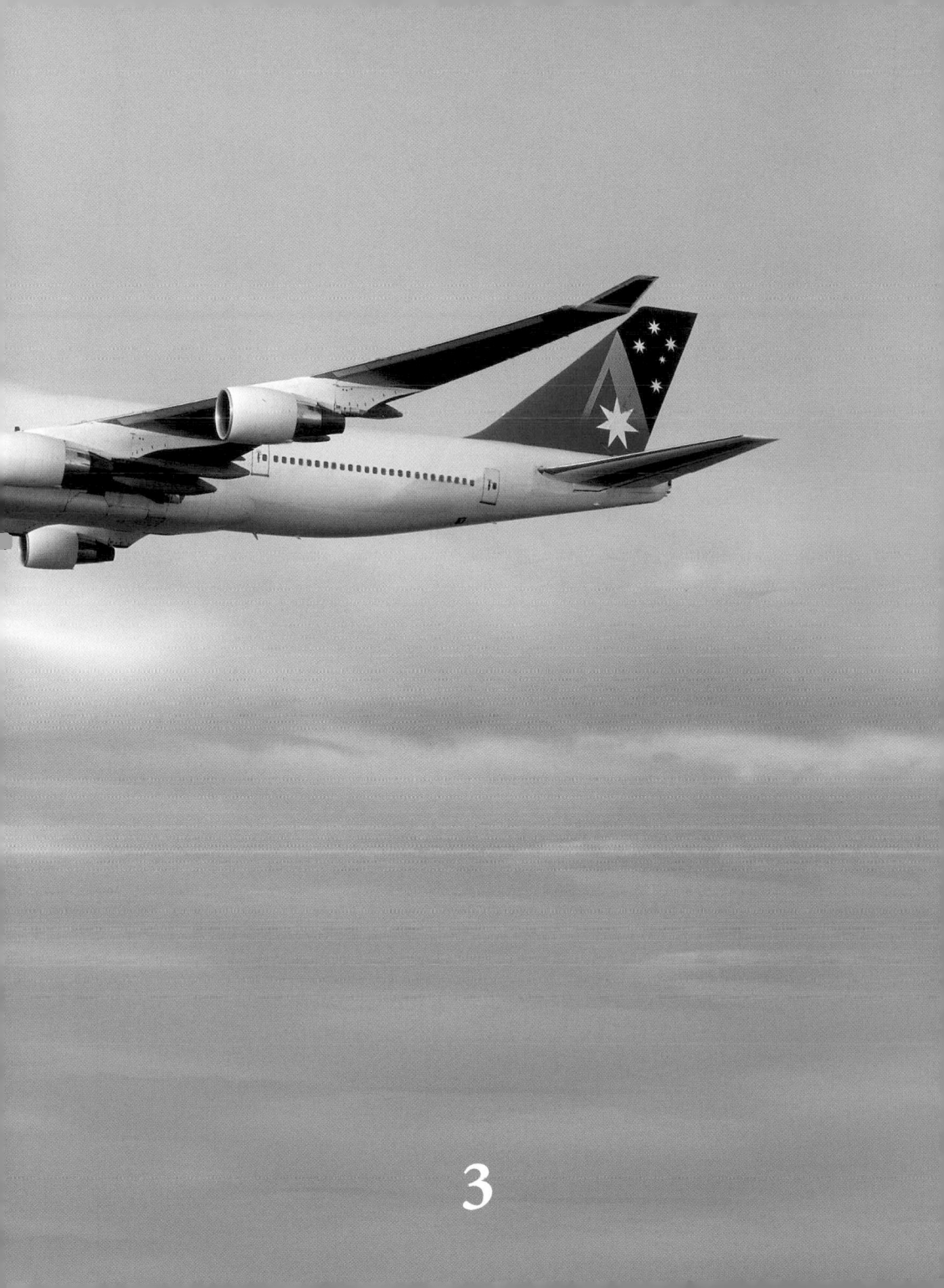

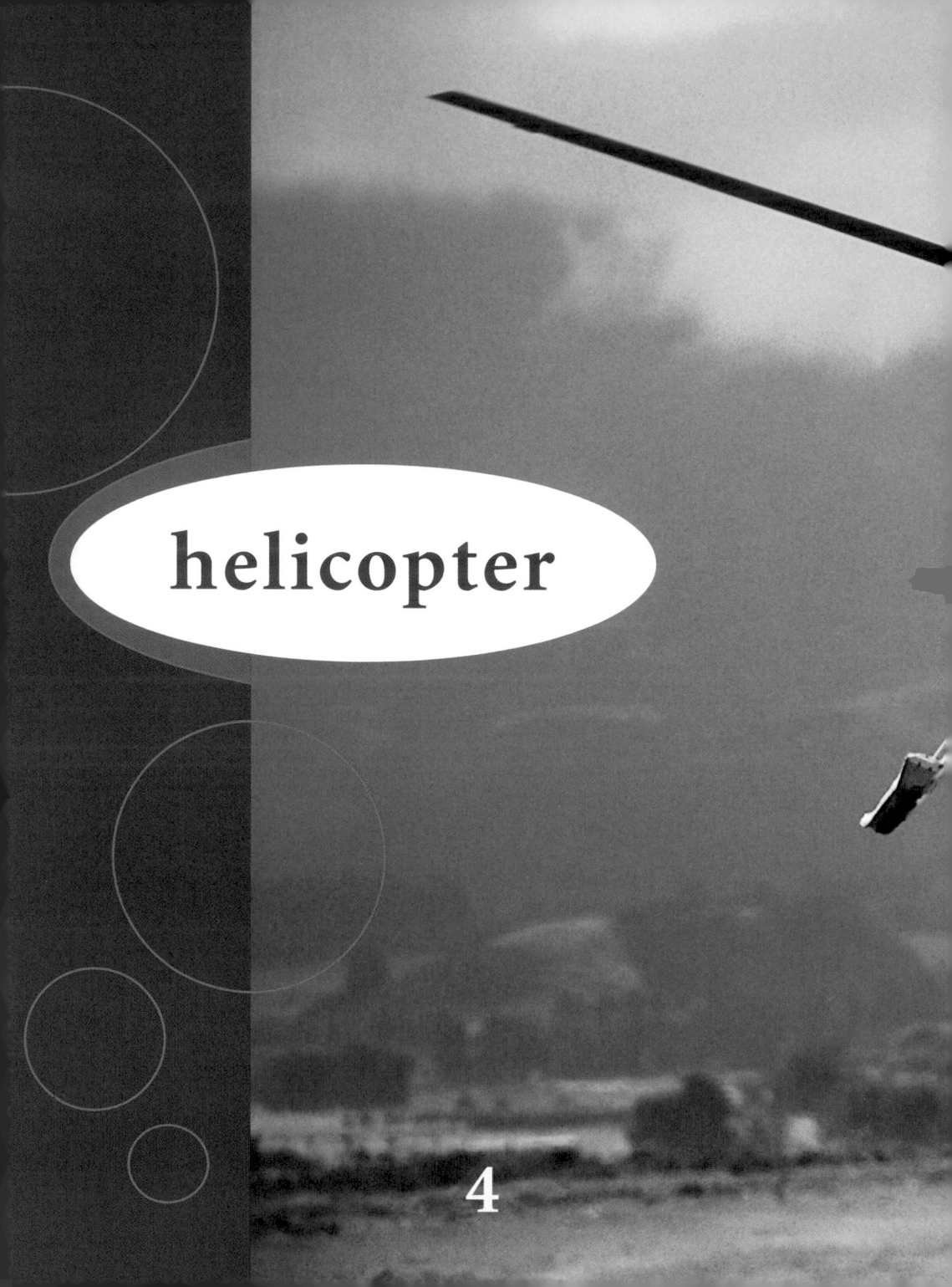

helicopter

4

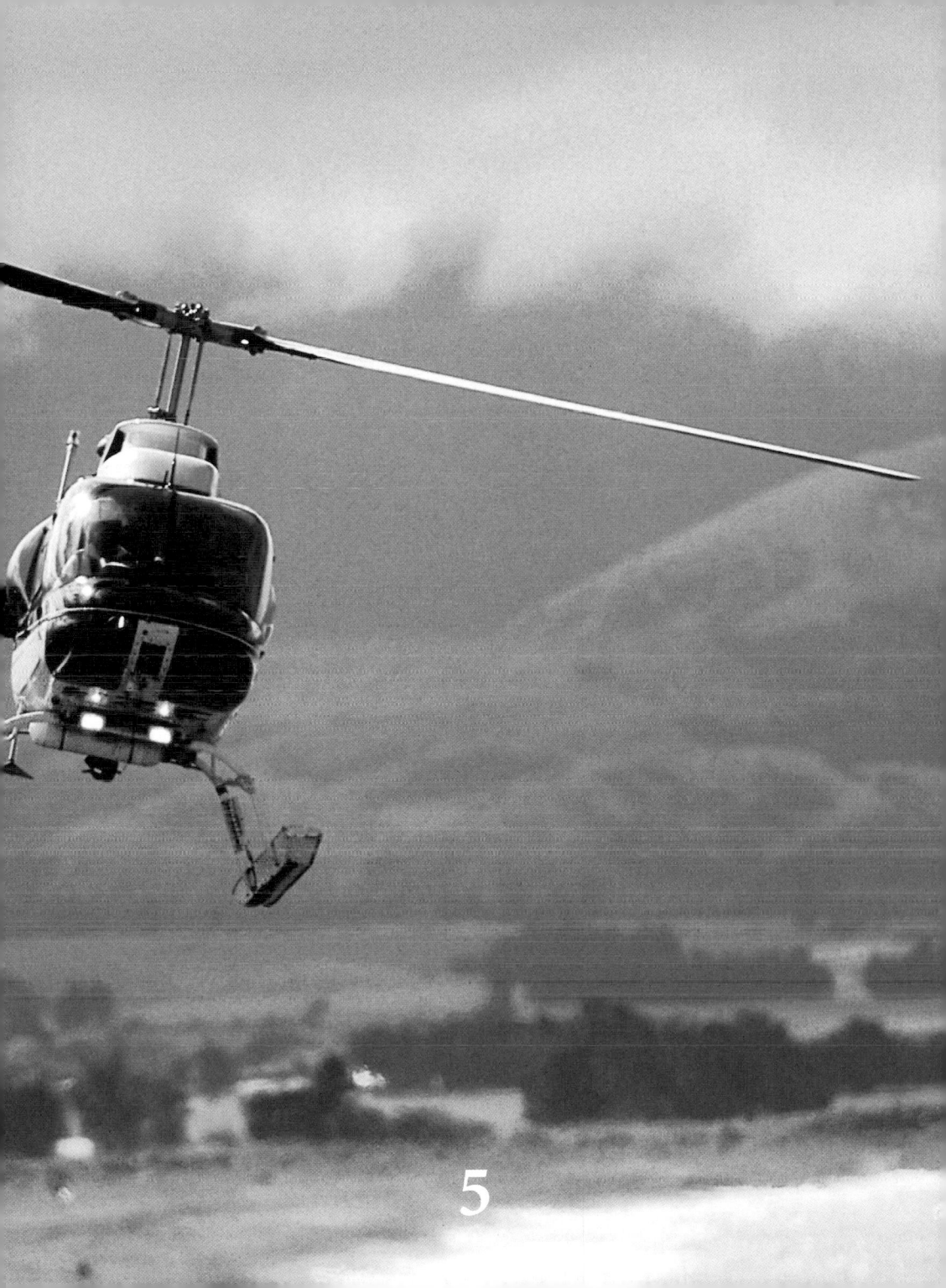

5

blimp

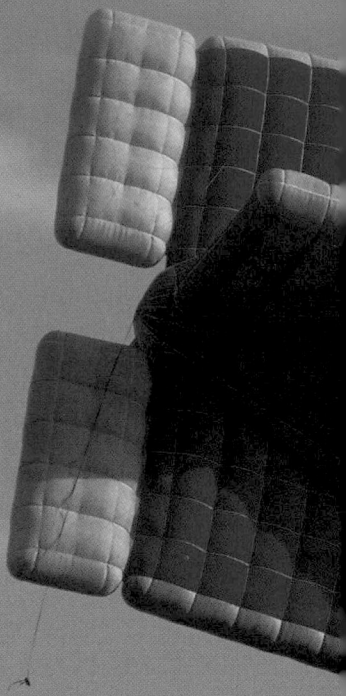

6

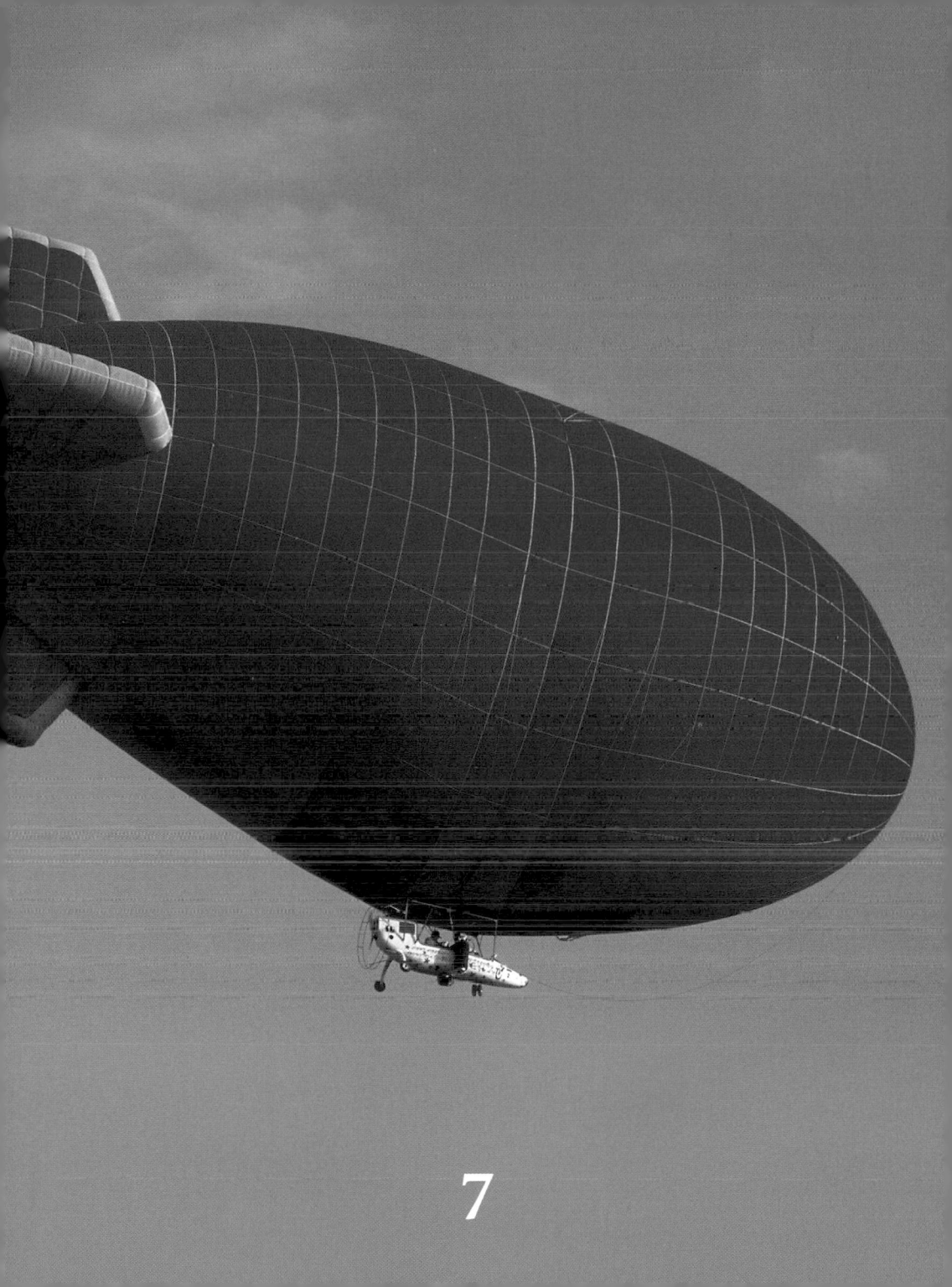

7

hot-air balloon

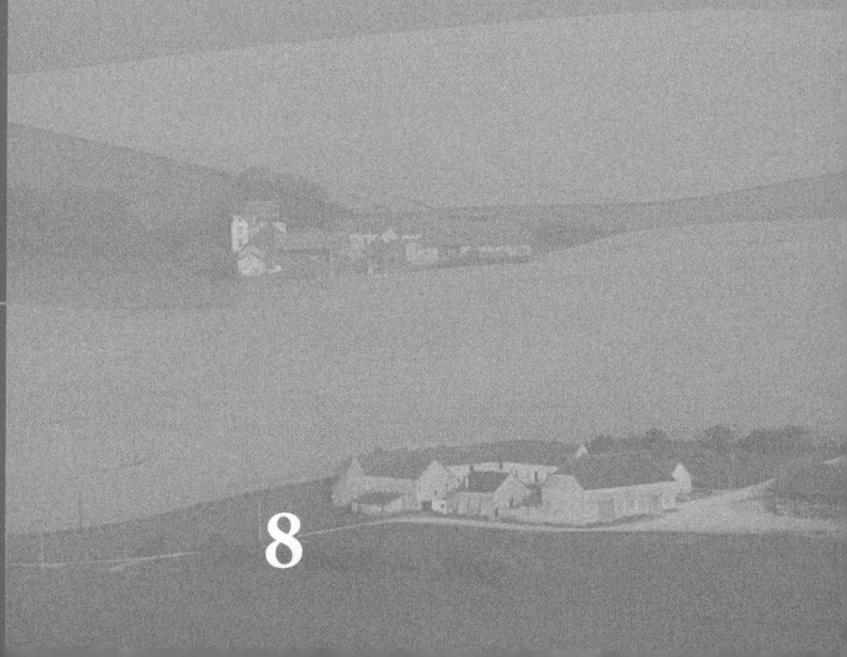

8

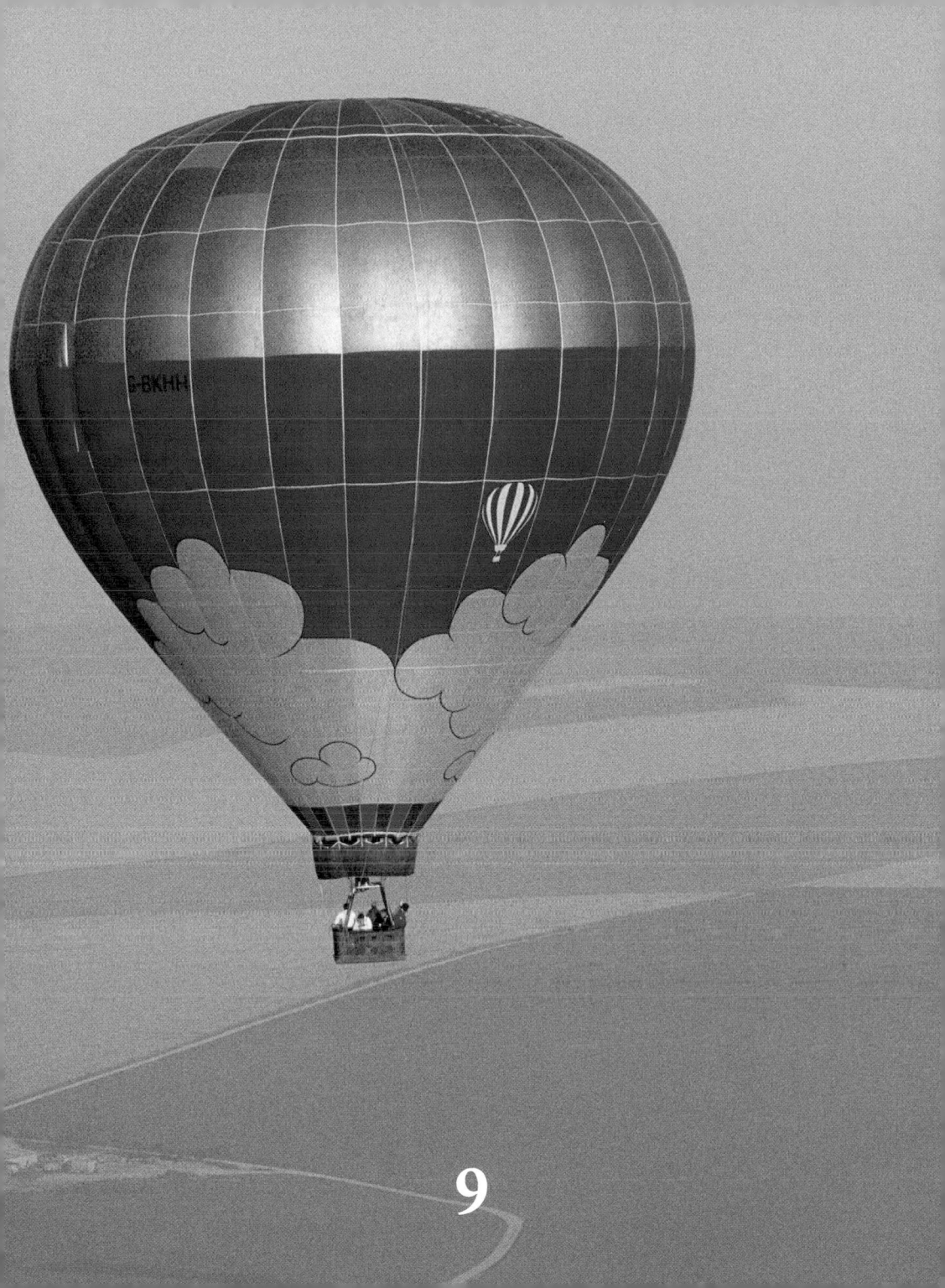

9

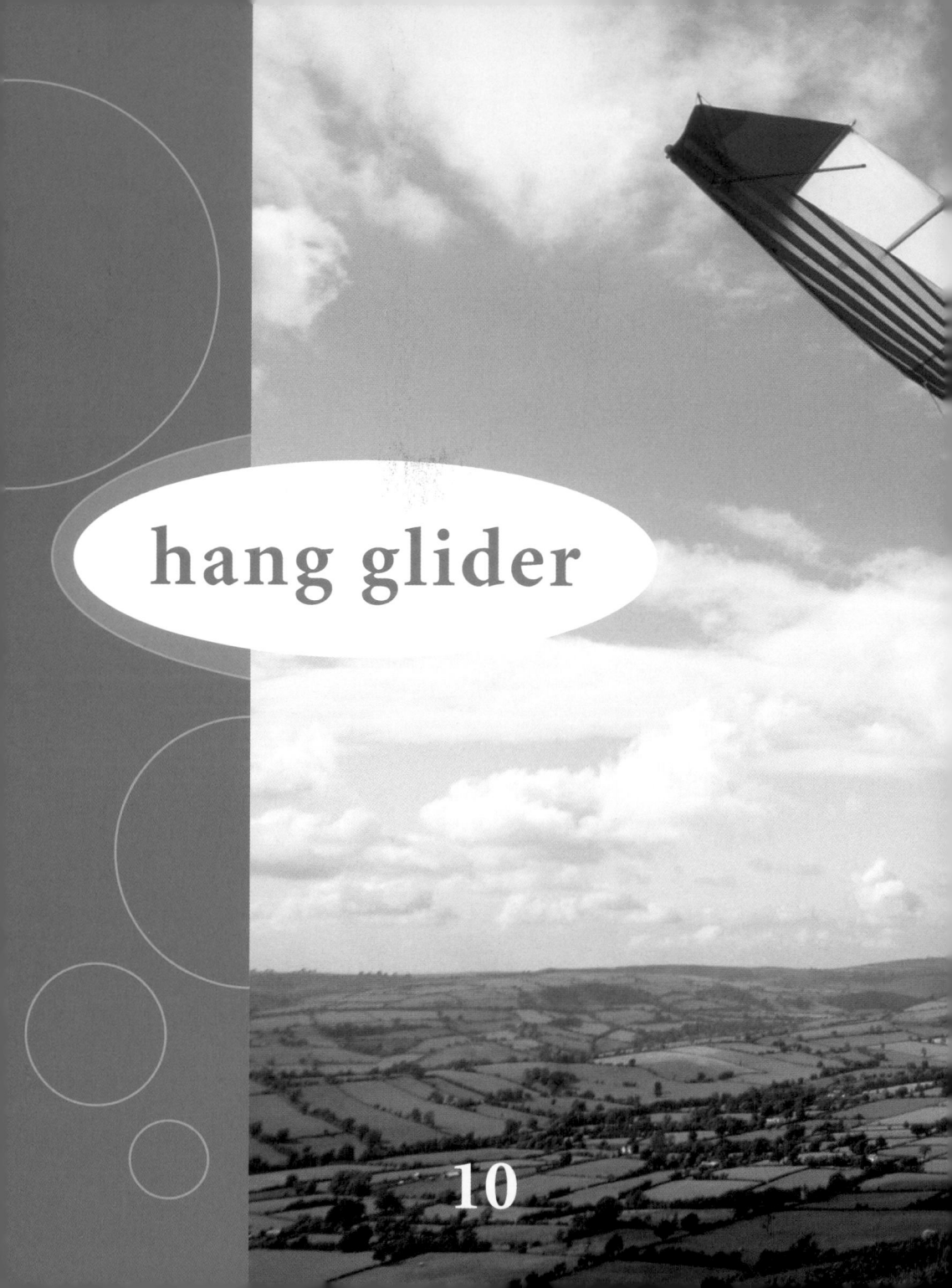

hang glider

10

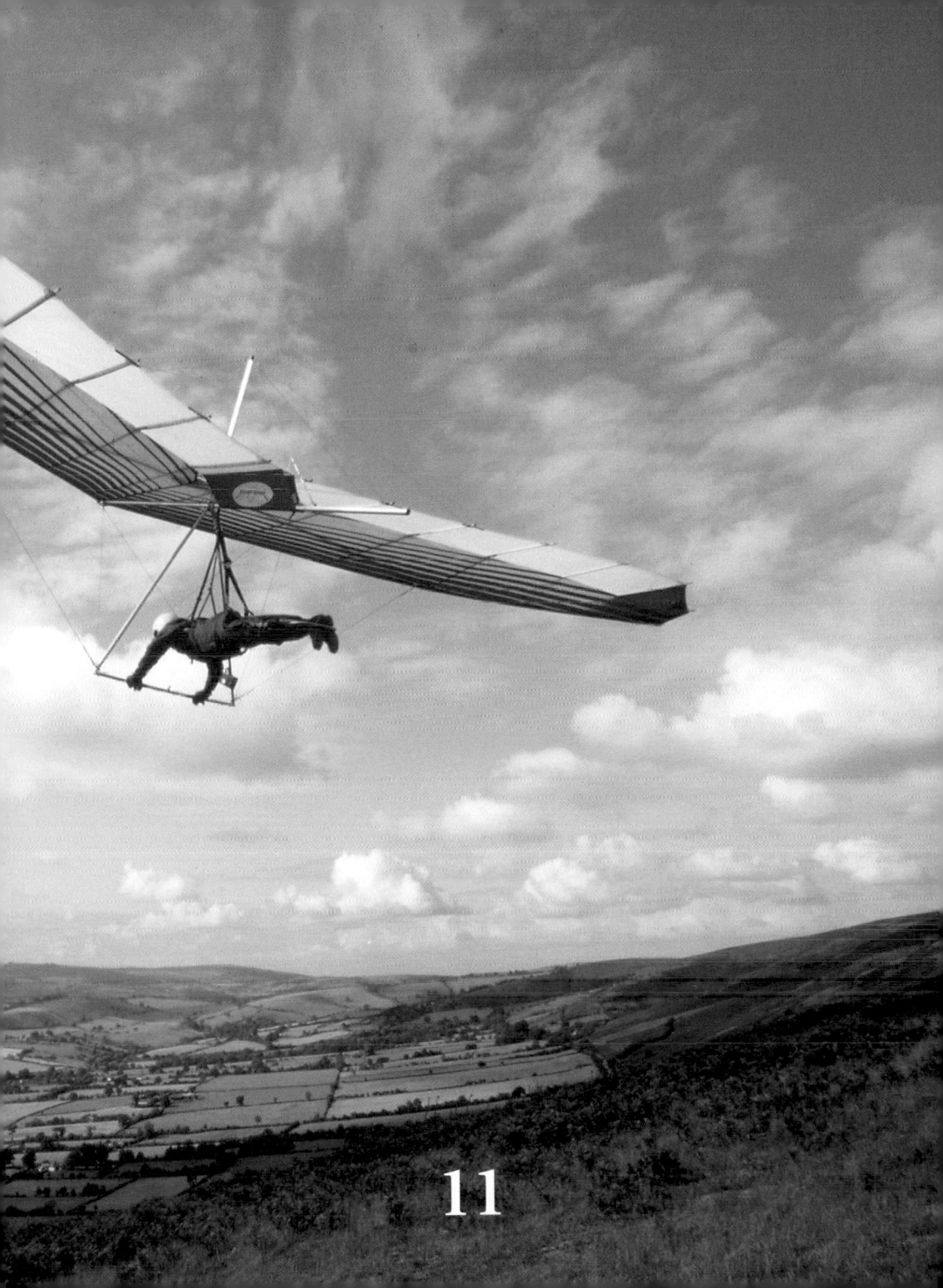

11

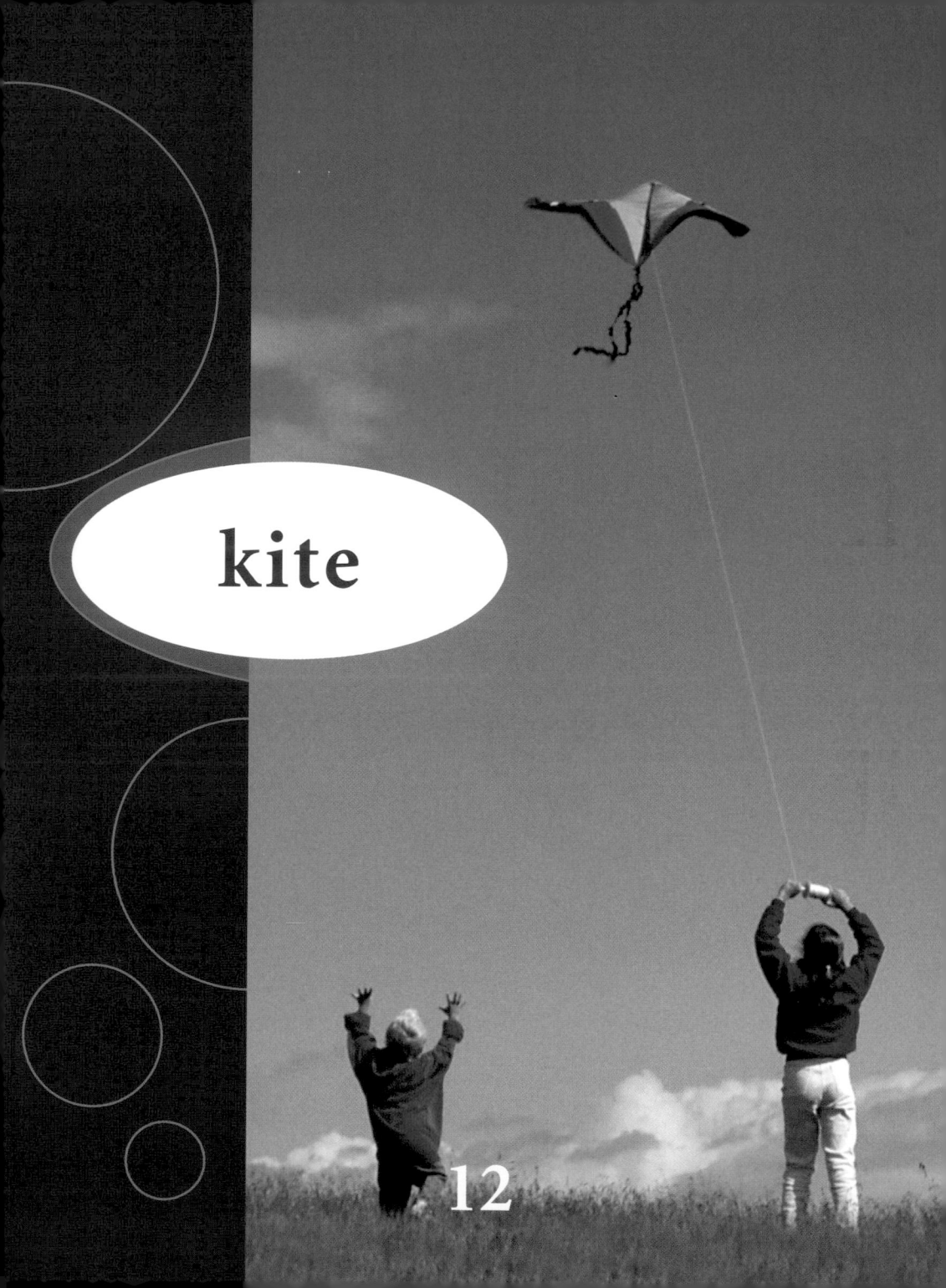

kite